How To Swim

Butterfly

a step-by-step guide for beginners
learning butterfly technique

Mark Young

Author Online!
For more resources and swimming help visit
Mark Young's website at

www.swim-teach.com

Mark Young is a well-established swimming instructor with over twenty years experience of teaching thousands of adults and children to swim. He has taken nervous, frightened children and adults with a fear of water and made them happy and confident swimmers.   He has also turned many of average ability into advanced swimmers. This book draws on his experiences and countless successes to put together this simplistic methodical approach to swimming.

Also by Mark Young

Step-By-Step Guides
How To Swim Breaststroke
How To Swim Backstroke
How To Swim Front Crawl

How To Be A Swimming Teacher
The Definitive Guide to Becoming a
Successful Swimming Teacher

A Catalogue record for this book is available from the British Library

ISBN 9780992742867

Published by: Educate & Learn Publishing, Hertfordshire, UK

Graphics by Mark Young, courtesy of Poser V6.0

Design and typeset by Mark Young

Published in association with www.swim-teach.com

Contents

How to use this book

Learning how to swim can be a frustrating experience sometimes, especially for an adult. Kick with your legs, pull with your arms, breathe in, and breathe out and do it all at the right time. Before you know it you've got a hundred and one things to think about and do all at the same time or in the right sequence.

How To Swim Butterfly is designed to break the stroke down into its component parts, those parts being body position, legs, arms, breathing and timing and coordination. An exercise or series of exercises are then assigned to that part along with relevant teaching points and technique tips, to help focus only on that stroke part.

The exercises form a reference section for the stroke, complete with technique tips, teaching points and common mistakes for each individual exercise.

What exactly are these exercises?

Each specific exercise focuses on a certain part of the swimming stroke, for example the body position, the leg kick, the arms, the breathing or the timing and coordination, all separated into easy to learn stages. Each one contains a photograph of the exercise being performed, a graphical diagram and all the technique elements and key focus points that are relevant to that particular exercise.

How will they help?

They break down your swimming technique into its core elements and then force you to focus on that certain area. For example if you are performing a leg kick exercise, the leg kick is isolated and therefore your focus and concentration is only on the legs. The technical information and key focus points then fix your concentration on the most important elements of the leg kick. The result: a more efficient and technically correct leg kick. The same then goes for exercises for the arms, breathing, timing and coordination and so on.

Will they help to learn and improve your swimming strokes?

Yes, definitely! Although it is not the same as having a swimming teacher with you to correct you, these practical exercises perfectly compliment lessons or help to enhance your practice time in the pool. They not only isolate certain areas but also can highlight your bad habits. Once you've worked though each element of the stroke and practiced the exercises a few times, you will slowly eliminate your bad habits. The result: a more efficient and technically correct swimming stroke, swum with less effort!

Butterfly

technique overview

Butterfly stroke is the most recent stroke, developed in the 1950's, and it is the second fastest stroke to Front Crawl. The stroke evolved from breaststroke as it also contains a simultaneous leg action and simultaneous arm action. The stroke requires a great deal of upper body strength and can be very physically demanding; therefore it is a stroke that is swum competitively rather than recreationally.

Buoyancy is very important because the arms are recovered over the water and the head is raised to breathe, therefore good floaters will achieve this far easier than poor floaters.

The timing and coordination of the stroke is usually a two beat cycle of leg kicks to one arm cycle.

The undulating action of the body and the legs create great demands of the spine, therefore there are many alternative exercises and practices that can be used to make learning the stroke easier and less physical.

Breathing is an explosive exhalation and then inhalation in the short second that the head and face are above the water surface.

The timing and coordination of butterfly is usually a two beat cycle of leg kicks to one arm cycle. One leg kick should have enough power to assist the upper body out and over the water surface and the second leg kick to assist the arms as they recover just over the surface of the water.

Body Position

The body position varies through the stroke cycle due to the continuous undulating action. The body should undulate from head to toe, producing a dolphin-type action.

Although undulation is unavoidable, the body position should be kept as horizontal as possible to keep frontal resistance to a minimum. Intermittent or alternative breathing will help to maintain this required body position.

The body should be face down (prone) with the crown of the head leading the action.

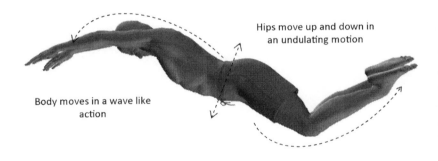

Hips move up and down in an undulating motion

Body moves in a wave like action

The shoulders should remain level throughout and the head should remain central and still, looking down until breathing is required.

Hips should be inline with the shoulders and should remain parallel to the direction of travel.

Common body position mistakes

The most common mistake made when performing the undulating movement is an excessive movement up and down. As the movement originates from the head there is a tendency to over exaggerate this movement, causing the wave movement through the rest of the body to excessive and over pronounced. The swimmer then puts more effort and energy into moving up and down instead of actually swimming forwards.

A simple push and glide exercise from the poolside followed by a gentle undulating movement across the surface of the water help to eliminate any excessive body movements.

If the swimmer places the effort on using the undulation to move forward then this will provide a solid base from which to build and perfect butterfly stroke.

Leg Kick

The main functions of butterfly stroke leg action are to balance the arm action and help to provide some propulsion. This action then generates the undulating movement of the body position as the swimmer moves through the water.

Simultaneous kick comes from the knee

Legs accelerate in an downbeat to provide propulsion

The legs kick simultaneously in an action that is similar to that of front crawl but with a greater and more pronounced knee bend.

The upbeat of the kick should come from the hip and the ankles should be relaxed with toes pointed. The legs move upwards without bending at the knees and the soles of the feet press against the water vertically and backwards.

Knees bend and then straighten on the downbeat to provide propulsion. The legs should accelerate to provide power on the downbeat.

Common leg kick mistakes

A breaststroke type leg kick can sometimes be performed by mistake, due to the simultaneous nature of the kick itself. Most swimmers that are able to perform breaststroke fairly well will naturally kick their legs in a small circle when attempting butterfly leg kick for the first time.

Another common mistake is to place an emphasis on the arm pull for butterfly and therefore lose all power from the leg kick. The legs just go through the motions when in fact they are needed to assist the body to rise out of the water so that the arm pull and recovery can be completed with minimum effort.

A powerful butterfly leg kick is vital and performing the kick whilst holding a float or kickboard out in front with straight arms will help develop the technique and power required for this movement.

Arms

Butterfly arm action is a continuous simultaneous movement that requires significant upper body strength. The action of the arms is similar to that of front crawl and the underwater catch, down sweep and upsweep parts draw the shape of a 'keyhole' through its movement path.

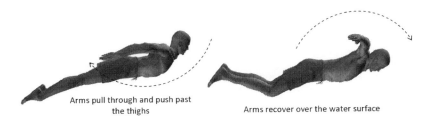

Arms pull through and push past the thighs

Arms recover over the water surface

Entry

The entry of the hands into the water should be fingertips first, leading with the thumb. Fingers should be together with palms flat and facing outwards. Arms should be stretched forward with a slightly bent elbow. Entry should be with arms extended inline with the shoulders.

Catch and down sweep

The pitch of the hands changes to a deeper angle with hands almost vertical. The catch and down sweep should begin just outside the shoulder line. Palms remain facing in the direction of travel. The elbow should bend to about 90 degrees to provide the extra power required. The hands sweep in a circular movement similar to breaststroke, but in a downward path.

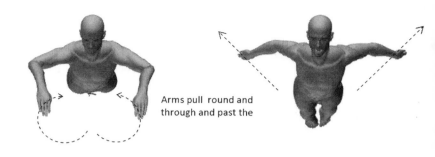

Arms pull round and
through and past the

Upsweep

The pitch of the hands changes to face out and upwards towards
the water surface. Elbows extend fully to straighten the arms and
hands towards the thighs.

Recovery

Hands and arms must clear the water on recovery in accordance
with ASA Law. Arms and hands should exit the water little finger
facing upwards. Arms must clear the surface as they are 'thrown'
over and forwards. Palms remain facing outwards, naturally
giving a thumb-first entry.

Common arm pull mistakes

The two most common mistakes made when it comes to
butterfly arm technique are an incomplete or short pull and a
wide hand entry.

The arm technique is sometimes compared to front crawl when it
is taught to beginners in its most basic form. This is due to the
long sweep and the recovery over the water surface. This is
where the similarities end and this comparison can sometimes be

taken literally, resulting in an almost double front crawl arm action with an excessive elbow bend.

The most common mistake made amongst slightly more advanced butterfly swimmers is a wide hand entry. The hands should enter the water inline with the shoulders. If the entry is wide of the shoulder line then this will result in a weak and inefficient arm pull.

Simply walking though shallow water of about shoulder depth practicing the arm action in slow motion will help to establish a full sweep and an inline hand entry.

Breathing

Breathing technique during butterfly is a rapid and explosive action.

Inhalation takes place as the arms complete their upsweep and begin to recover, as the body begins to rise. The head is lifted enough for the mouth to clear the water and the chin should be pushed forward, but remain at the water surface. Some exhalation underwater takes place during this phase.

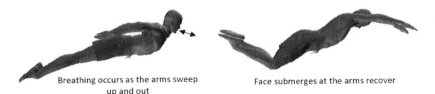

Breathing occurs as the arms sweep up and out

Face submerges at the arms recover

The head is lowered quickly into the water again as the arms recover inline with the shoulders, to resume an overall streamlined position and maintain minimal frontal resistance.

Explosive breathing is normally preferred but a combination of trickle and explosive breathing can be used. Explosive breathing involves a rapid exhalation followed immediately by inhalation, requiring powerful use of the respiratory muscles.

Common breathing mistakes

Failure to actually breathe is the most common mistake made by beginners learning butterfly breathing technique.

Because the inhalation and exhalation have to take place very quickly in the short second the face is being raised, it is very common to either inhale only or not breathe at all. The result: a pair of extremely inflated lungs and a severe lack of oxygen.

Performing the full stroke and taking a breath every other stroke cycle is a good way of ensuring that exhalation is taking place and that the lungs are sufficiently emptied before inhalation takes place.

Timing

The butterfly stroke cycle should contain 2 leg kicks to 1 arm cycle where the first kick occurs when the arms are forward and the second kick when the have pulled back.

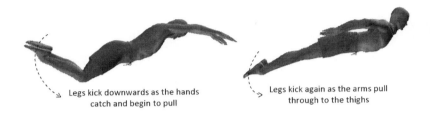

Legs kick downwards as the hands catch and begin to pull

Legs kick again as the arms pull through to the thighs

The downbeat of the first leg kick occurs at the catch and down sweep phase. Both arms will have been in the air during recovery, causing the hips to sink. The subsequent kick should be strong enough to counter balance this hip movement.

The second downbeat leg kick occurs during the powerful and accelerating upsweep phase of the arm cycle. During this movement, the feet react towards the hands and the strength will contribute towards propulsion.

Breathing can occur every stroke cycle or every other stroke cycle.

Common timing mistakes

Timing and coordination issues can occur when the swimmer attempts to kick and pull at the same time. There should be a delay from the leg kick as the arms pull, so that the first powerful leg kick assists the arms recovery.

Beginners learning butterfly tend to miss out the second supporting leg kick as the arms recover.

A good way to practice and develop the timing for this stroke is to swim using a butterfly leg kick and a breaststroke arm pull. There is less energy used when swimming with breaststroke arms because the arms recover under the water surface. Therefore it is an ideal way to ensure that there are two leg kicks for each arm pull, where one leg kick assists the body to rise and breathe, and the other smaller leg kick assists the arms to recover.

Once this exercise is perfected then the swimmer can reintroduce butterfly arms into the stroke and maintain the timing and coordination pattern.

Butterfly

exercises

BUTTERFLY: Body Position

Holding the poolside

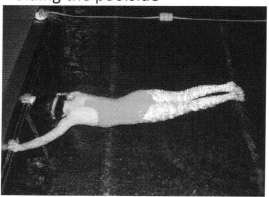

Aim: to practise the body position and movement by holding on to the poolside.

The swimmer performs an undulating action whilst using the poolside or rail for support. Note: this exercise should be performed slowly and without force or power as the static nature places pressure on the lower back.

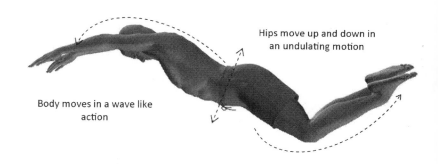

Hips move up and down in an undulating motion

Body moves in a wave like action

Key Actions
Keep your head in the middle
Make the top of your head lead first
Keep your shoulders level
Keep your hips level
Make your body into a long wave

Technical Focus
Exercise should be slow and gradual
Head remains central
Shoulders and hips should be level
Horizontal body with an undulating movement
Wave like movement from head to toe
Legs remain together

Common Faults
Body remains too stiff and rigid
Head moves to the sides
Shoulders and hips are not remaining level

BUTTERFLY: Body Position

Dolphin dives

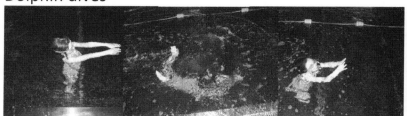

Aim: to develop an undulating body movement whilst travelling through water of standing depth.
The swimmer performs a series of dives from a standing position, diving deep under the surface, arching the back and resurfacing immediately to stand up. The aim is to perform as many dolphin dives across the width as possible. Swimmers can then progress to performing the practice without standing in-between dives.

Body dives down and then resurfaces immediately in a wave like movement

Key Actions
Keep your head in the middle
Make the top of your head dive down first
Make your body into a huge wave
Stretch up to the surface

Technical Focus
Head remains central
Shoulders and hips should be level
Body moves with an undulating movement
Wave-like movement from head to toe
Legs remain together

Common Faults
Body remains too stiff and rigid
Body dives but fails to undulate upwards
Leading with the head looking forwards

BUTTERFLY: Body Position

Push and glide

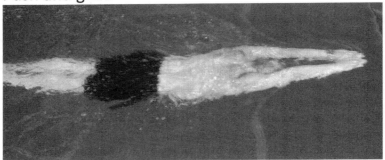

Aim: to practise and develop an undulating action whilst moving.

The swimmer pushes from the poolside into a glide and then begins the undulating action from head to toe. This allows the swimmer to experience the required undulating action whilst moving through the water.

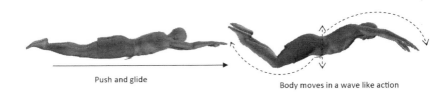

Push and glide

Body moves in a wave like action

Key Actions
Make the top of your head lead first
Keep your shoulders level
Keep your hips level
Make your body into a long wave
Pretend you are a dolphin swimming

Technical Focus
Head remains central
Shoulders and hips should be level
Body is horizontal with an undulating movement
Wave-like movement from head to toe
Legs remain together

Common Faults
Body remains too stiff and rigid
Shoulders and hips are not remaining level
Leading with the head looking forwards

BUTTERFLY: Legs

Sitting on the poolside

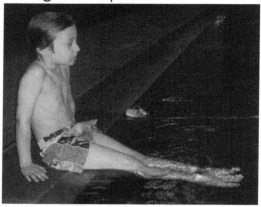

Aim: to develop the kicking action whilst sitting on the poolside.

Bending and kicking from the knees with legs together allows the swimmer to practise the correct movement and feel the water at the same time.

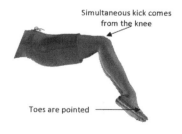

Simultaneous kick comes from the knee

Toes are pointed

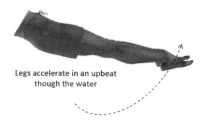

Legs accelerate in an upbeat though the water

Key Actions
Kick both legs at the same time
Keep your ankles loose
Keep your legs together
Point your toes

Technical Focus
Simultaneous legs action
Knees bend and kick in upbeat to provide propulsion
Legs accelerate on upbeat
Toes are pointed

Common Faults
Leg kick is not simultaneous
Toes are not pointed
Overall action is too stiff and rigid
Kick is not deep or powerful enough

BUTTERFLY: Legs

Push and glide adding leg kick

Aim: to practise the dolphin leg kick action and experience movement.

This allows the swimmer the develop propulsion from the accelerating leg kick and undulating body movement.

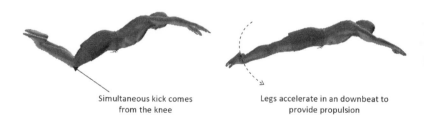

Simultaneous kick comes from the knee

Legs accelerate in an downbeat to provide propulsion

Key Actions
Keep your ankles loose
Kick downwards powerfully
Keep your legs together
Point your toes
Kick like a mermaid

Technical Focus
Simultaneous legs action
Knees bend and kick in downbeat to provide propulsion
Legs accelerate on downbeat
Toes are pointed
Hips initiate undulating movement

Common Faults
Leg kick is not simultaneous
Toes are not pointed
Overall action is too stiff and rigid
Kick is not deep or powerful enough

BUTTERFLY: Legs

Prone holding a float with both hands

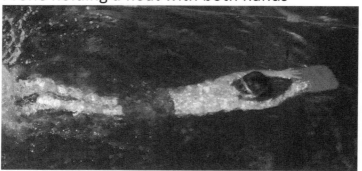

Aim: to develop the leg kick using a float for support.

This practice allows the advanced swimmer to develop leg kick strength and stamina as the float isolates the legs.

Powerful leg kick provides propulsion and help the body to undulate

Key Actions
Kick with both legs at the same time
Kick downwards powerfully
Keep your legs together
Create a wave-like action through your body
Kick like a mermaid

Technical Focus
Simultaneous legs action
Knees bend and kick in downbeat to provide propulsion
Legs accelerate on downbeat
Toes are pointed
Hips initiate undulating movement

Common Faults
Leg kick is not simultaneous
Toes are not pointed
Overall action is too stiff and rigid
Kick is not deep or powerful enough

BUTTERFLY: Legs

Supine position with arms by sides

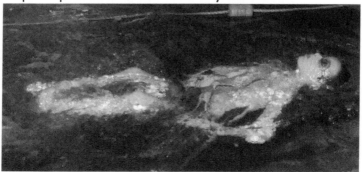

Aim: to practise and develop a dolphin leg kick action in a supine position.

This allows the swimmer to kick continuously whilst facing upwards. This practice requires a great deal of leg strength and stamina and therefore is ideal for developing these aspects of the stroke.

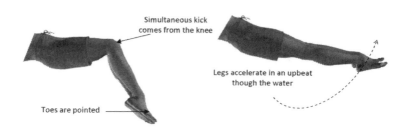

Simultaneous kick comes from the knee

Legs accelerate in an upbeat though the water

Toes are pointed

Key Actions
Kick both legs at the same time
Keep your ankles loose
Kick upwards powerfully
Keep your legs together
Point your toes

Technical Focus
Simultaneous legs action
Knees bend and kick in upbeat to provide propulsion
Legs accelerate on upbeat
Toes are pointed
Hips initiate undulating movement

Common Faults
Leg kick is not simultaneous
Overall action is too stiff and rigid
Hips are not undulating to initiate the kick
Kick is not deep or powerful enough

BUTTERFLY: Legs

Kick and roll

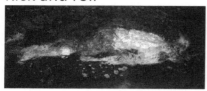 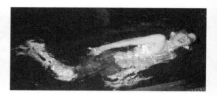

Aim: to combine the leg kick and undulating body movement and perform a rolling motion through the water.

This practice can be performed with arms held by the sides or held out in front. The rolling motion forces the swimmer to use the head, shoulders and hips to produce the movement required for powerful undulating propulsion.

Legs kick and body performs a 'cork screw' like roll through the water

Key Actions
Kick both legs at the same time
Keep your ankles loose
Roll like a corkscrew
Keep your legs together
Make your body snake through the water

Technical Focus
Simultaneous legs action
Head and shoulders initiate rolling motion
Knees bend and kick to provide propulsion
Legs accelerate on downbeat
Hips initiate undulating movement

Common Faults
Leg kick is not simultaneous
Overall action is too stiff and rigid
Kick is not powerful enough

BUTTERFLY: Arms

Standing on the poolside

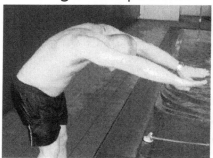 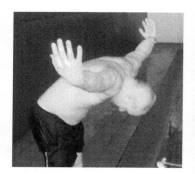

Aim: to practise correct butterfly arm action whilst standing on the poolside.

The pupil is able to work through the arm action slowly and in stages so as to experience the basic movement required.

Arms pull through in a keyhole shape

Arms pull through and past the thighs

Key Actions
Move both arms at the same time
Thumbs go in first
Draw a keyhole under your body
Push past your thighs

Technical Focus
Arms move simultaneously
Hands enter the water in line with the shoulders
Hands pull in the shape of a keyhole
Hands push past the thigh

Common Faults
Arm action is not simultaneous
Arms are too straight
Arms are not pulling back to the thighs

BUTTERFLY: Arms

Walking on the pool floor

Aim: to progress from the previous practice and develop the arm action.

The swimmer can get a feel for the water whilst walking and performing the simultaneous arm action.

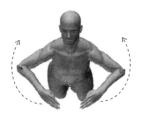

Arms pull through simultaneously

Arms are thrown forwards over the water surface

Key Actions
Move both arms at the same time
Thumbs go in first
Draw a keyhole under your body
Push past your thighs

Technical Focus
Arms move simultaneously
Hands enter the water in line with the shoulders
Hands pull in the shape of a keyhole
Hands push past the thigh

Common Faults
Arm action is not simultaneous
Arms are too straight
Fingers are apart
Hands fail to clear the water

BUTTERFLY: Arms

Push and glide adding arms

Aim: to practise the arm action whilst moving through the water.

Correct body position is established from the push and glide and the swimmer can then use the arm action to maintain momentum through the water. A limited number of arm pulls can be achieved with this practice.

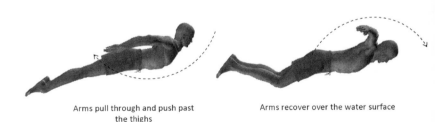

Arms pull through and push past the thighs

Arms recover over the water surface

Key Actions

Move both arms at the same time
Thumbs enter water first
Pull hard through the water
Pull past your thighs
Throw your arms over the water

Technical Focus

Arms move simultaneously
Fingers closed together
Thumbs enter the water first
Hands enter the water in line with the shoulders
Hands push past the thigh
Hands clear water surface on recovery

Common Faults

Arms are too straight
Arms are not pulling back to the thighs
Hands fail to clear the water

BUTTERFLY: Arms

Arms only using a pull-buoy

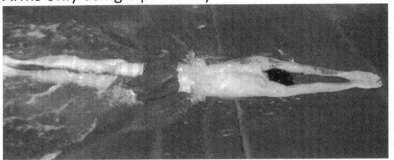

Aim: to help the swimmer develop arm strength and stamina.

This practice is performed over a longer distance, progressing from the previous practice. The pull buoy provides buoyancy and support as well as helps the undulating body movement.

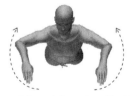

Arms pull through the water with power

Hands and arms clear the water on recovery

Key Actions

Thumbs go in first
Pull hard through the water
Pull past your thighs
Throw your arms over the water

Technical Focus

Arms move simultaneously
Fingers closed together
Thumbs enter the water first
Hands enter the water in line with the shoulders
Hands push past the thigh
Hands clear water surface on recovery

Common Faults

Arms are too straight
Arms are not pulling back to the thighs
Hands fail to clear the water

BUTTERFLY: Arms

Arm action with breaststroke leg kicks

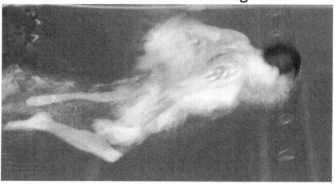

Aim: to enable use of breaststroke leg kicks to support the arm action.

As the legs kick, the propulsion helps the body to rise and the arms to recover over the water surface. This practice is also a good introduction to the timing of butterfly arms and legs.

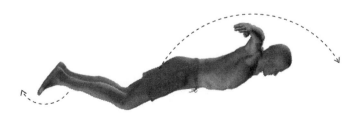

Leg kick help the arms to recover over the water surface

Key Actions
Thumbs go in first
Draw a keyhole under your body
Pull past your thighs
Little finger comes out first
Throw your arms over the water

Technical Focus
Thumbs enter the water first
Hands pull in the shape of a keyhole
Hands push past the thigh
Little finger exits the water first
Hands clear water surface on recovery

Common Faults
Arms are too straight
Arms are not pulling back to the thighs
Fingers are apart
Hands fail to clear the water

BUTTERFLY: Breathing

Standing breathing, with arm pulls

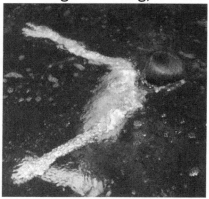

Aim: to incorporate butterfly breathing into the arm action.

This practice is performed standing either on the poolside or stationary in water of standing depth.

Breathing occurs as the arms sweep up and out

Face submerges at the arms recover

Key Actions
Blow out hard as your chin rises
Put your face down as your arms recover
Push your chin forward and breathe every arm pull or every two
    arm pulls

Technical Focus
Breathing in should occur as the arms sweep up and out
Explosive breathing is most beneficial
Chin should remain in the water
Face dives into the water as the arms come level with the
    shoulders
Breath can be taken every stroke cycle or alternate cycles

Common Faults
Lifting the head too high
Arms stop recovery to breathe
Holding the breath

BUTTERFLY: Breathing

Full stroke

Aim: to use the full stroke to practice breathing, incorporating regular breaths into the arm and leg actions.

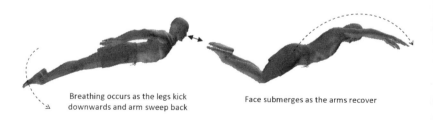

Breathing occurs as the legs kick downwards and arm sweep back

Face submerges as the arms recover

Key Actions
Blow out hard as your chin rises
Lift your head to breathe in as your legs kick down
Put your face down as your arms come over
Push your chin forward and breathe every arm pull or every two
arm pulls

Technical Focus
Breathing in occurs as the arms sweep upwards
Breathing in occurs as the legs are kicking downwards
Explosive breathing is most beneficial
Chin remains in the water
Face dives into the water as the arms come level with the
shoulders
Breath can be taken every stroke cycle or alternate cycles

Common Faults
Lifting the head too high
Arms stop recovery to breathe
Holding the breath
Breathing too often

BUTTERFLY: Timing

Full stroke

Aim: to perform the full stroke butterfly, incorporating two leg kicks per arm pull.

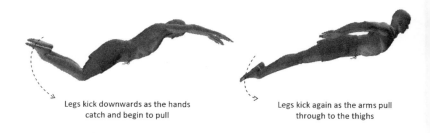

Legs kick downwards as the hands
catch and begin to pull

Legs kick again as the arms pull
through to the thighs

Key Actions
Kick hard as your hands enter the water
Kick again as your hands pull under your body

Technical Focus
Two legs kicks per arm cycle
Legs kick once as hands enter and sweep out
Legs kick once as arms sweep up and out

Common Faults
Only kicking once per arm cycle
Kicking too many times per arm cycle

"Now that you have finished my book, would you please consider writing a review? Reviews are the best way readers discover great new books. I would truly appreciate it."

Mark Young

For more information about learning to swim and improving your swimming strokes and swimming technique visit:

swim-teach.com

"The number one resource for learning to swim and improving swimming technique."

www.swim-teach.com

Printed in Great Britain
by Amazon